D1060520

Published under the copyright laws of the
Library of Congress of the United States of
America by:
Orthotic Interventions
Oakbrook Terrace, IL 60181
International STandard Book Number
(ISBN):
978-0-9975102-0-1

ANIMALS AMONG US

Dedicated to Olivia and Emma
with love.

Story: Dulcey and Sarah Lima
Photos: Dulcey Lima
Editors: Sarah and Skip Lima

Pipevine Swallowtails love to search.

On sweet summer flowers, they will perch.

The Morton Arboretum, Lisle, IL

Look at the Eastern Swallowtail's wings!
They flit and flutter over meadows and springs.

Meadowlark Botanic Garden
Vienna, VA

The Monarch Caterpillar is wiggly as can be,
Then it turns into a Butterfly and is a sight to see.

Here in an instant, there in a blink!
This Hummingbird is looking for flowers to drink.

Ventana Canyon
Tucson, AZ

Tree Swallows
fly in turns and
twists,

To eat flying
insects in our
midst.

The Morton Arboretum
Lisle, IL

Mr. Cardinal, is there any bird redder than you?

Your color attracts females when it's time to woo.

Ventana Canyon
Tucson, AZ

Wild Turkeys fan out their feathers and gobble. When two turkeys get together, they sometimes squabble.

The Gardens at Cantigny Park
Winfield, IL

The Blue Footed Booby of Galapagos fame,
Has bright blue feet—thus its name!

The Galapagos Islands
Ecuador

This Great Blue Heron's
one big wish,
Is to catch and eat this
little fish.

Fort Myers Beach
FL

Brown Pelicans soar in
skies so blue,

They must have the
most wonderful view!

Fort Myers Beach
FL

These Great Horned Owlets are too young to fly.
Their parents still feed them when they pass by.

Fabyan Park
Geneva, IL

The Turkey Vulture looks for dead animals to eat.
It cleans up the ecosystem by this very feat.

Lover's Key
Bonita Springs, FL

Anhingas use their
very sharp beaks,

To spear little fish
in swampy creeks.

Corkscrew Swamp
Naples, FL

Most Iguanas only crawl on land.
But this Marine Iguana likes water and sand.

The Galapagos Islands
Ecuador

Alligators are reptiles that are very strong.
Their bodies can be up to 13 feet long.

Bird Rookery Swamp
Naples, FL

What's all that croaking you hear in the bog?
It's the sound of a green and slippery frog.

The Gardens at Cantigny Park
Winfield, IL

Adult Galapagos Tortoises can weigh 500 pounds.
They move very slowly across the ground.

The Galapagos Islands
Ecuador

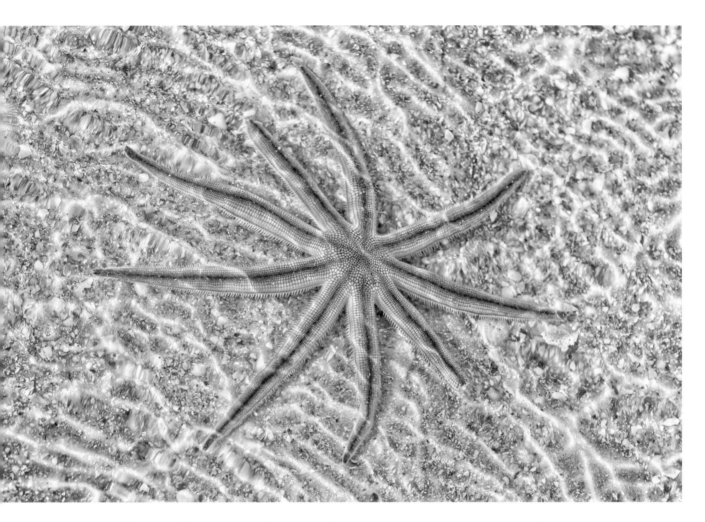

Reach, reach, with arms open wide.
That's the way a Sea Star rides on the tide.

Fort Myers Beach
FL

Sally Lightfoot Crabs scuttle over rocks and sea.
Their vivid, bright colors are lovely to me.

The Galapagos Islands
Ecuador

Hey, Kangaroo! Some advice for you:

Don't slouch,

Or your
pouch,

Will flop,

When you
hop!

Kangaroo Island
Australia

The Koala climbs
trees and eats
eucalyptus.

To us that seems
yucky, but to her
it's delicious!

Kangaroo Island
Australia

Through the trees
a Monkey can sail,

Using four limbs
and its prehensile
tail.

Manuel Antonio National Park
Costa Rica

The Leopard can run 35 miles per hour.
Its legs are quite strong and they give it great power.

Chicago Zoological Society
Brookfield, IL

Gorillas are Apes--big and strong.
Smart and social--to their groups they belong.

Lincoln Park Zoo
Chicago, IL

A Mountain Lion can leap more than 18 feet high.
The sheer size of this animal can terrify!

Sonora Desert Museu
Tucson, AZ

A Tiger is
orange and its
stripes are black.

It uses its nose
and its sharp
ears to track.

Naples Zoo at Caribbean Gardens,
Naples, FL

Rhinos are big animals with horns on their faces.
Thick skin gives them protection in all the right place

Lincoln Park Zoo
Chicago, IL

Burros are small donkeys that live in the heat.
Desert plants and small shrubs are what they like to
eat.

Red Rock Canyon
Las Vegas, NV

Bighorn Sheep climb mountains and are sure-footed and strong.
Their horns are curvy and really quite long.

Giraffes are very tall and eat leaves from the trees.

With their long necks they do this with the greatest of ease.

Naples Zoo and Caribbean Gardens
Naples, FL

Sea Lions are mammals that live in the ocean.
They make lots of sounds that raise quite a
commotion.

The Galapagos Islands
Ecuador

Coyotes look doglike and at night they prowl.
To communicate with each other they usually howl.

Ventana Canyon
Tucson, AZ

A Jack Rabbit is a Hare with very long ears.
It can hop away fast if there is something it fears.

A Calico Cat has tricolored fur.
Petting her yields a warm, friendly purr.

Cincinnati, OH

A Dog is said to be a human's best friend.
It's loyalty and devotion will never end.

Haymarket, VA

We're grateful for all animals--big and small. Some fly through the air, swim the seas, or crawl. They have different faces, and live in vast places.

We'll protect them to make earth a safe place for all.

CPSIA information can be obtained at www.ICGtesting.com
Printed in the USA
LVIW01n1512280916
506565LV00026B/325

* 9 7 8 0 9 9 7 5 1 0 2 0 1 *